Blues Blood

Robert Earl Price

Blues Blood

new and selected poems

Alexis,

much respect & gratitude for your creative contribution to Yardbird.

Peace & Power

Robert - Bashiri

4 Nov. 99 - Berlin

CAC Press
Atlanta, GA, USA
1994

Manufactured in Atlanta, GA, USA.
Cover design by Gail Tassell.
Printed at TransAmerica Printing (Downtown), Atlanta, GA with many thanks to Gisele and John Price, Joe, Kip and Scott.
Cover art by C. Colgate.

Some of these poems were first published in reviews, magazines and chapbooks. I am grateful to Togetherness Press, Poetry Atlanta, *Snake Nation Review*, *Catalyst* and all of the editors who have so graciously granted permission to revise and reprint.

Much appreciation to the many writers who have shaped my song including Amiri Baraka, Aimé Césaire, Henry Dumas, Felton Eaddy, Nicolás Guillén, Larry Neal, Eugene B. Redmond, Askia M. Touré, the two Toni's, Alice Walker and Margaret Walker.

Library of Congress Catalog Card Number: 94-72477
Price, Robert Earl. **Blues Blood**

ISBN 0-9642183-0-5

CAC Press, PO Box 5258, Atlanta, GA 31107

Dedicated to
my mom, Theodus B. Hankerson
my son, Dhaiti Haile Price
and all those engaged in the struggle of
memory against forgetting.

Contents

The bird with feathers once more beautiful
than the past
demands an accounting for its scattered
plumes

Aimé Césaire

I am a Black man.
The Yagruma
of snow and emerald
beneath the moon.

Nicolás Guillén

They will ask you your name
and where you got your sound.
Tell 'em you got it being
mean and low down.

Larry Neal

Poetry

In the beginning was the word
and the word was poetry
A direct wire from heart to spirit
The mind coming to hear
what has always been
Truth on the lips of snakes
Love weeping by the river's edge
Genius on a twelve story ledge
A poet in the throes

In the beginning was the word
and the word was poetry
A sign from some perfect place
Neither word nor song
An ambience from Eden
Ojenka stammering out judgement
Kamau howling outside the temple
Bashiri witness to daybreak
Poets are like fish in the blood

In the beginning was the word
and the word was poetry
A potion for the soul
A jeweled cog in the great machine
Danger to the present
Threat to the liar
Anarchy and revolt trail poets
around like the scent of ginger bread

In the beginning was the word
and the word was poetry
which was many words
while it was still the word
It is my neon heartbeat
Screams from a dark and icy tenement
Blood sizzling on the griddle
No time but now
No home but here
No word but one
Poetry...Poetry...Poetry
Captured me
Drove me mad
in all tenses

Souped Blues

men don't like me
 cause I always speak my mind
women crazy about me
 cause I always take my time

born on a bottle neck scream
raised in a gut bucket hollow
Lawdy, Lawdy, Lawdy
blues been bred in my blood
guitars and saxophones sewn in my genes
Blind Willie McTell rocked my cradle
Son House trained my traveling pony
I'm the one they called the 7th son
famous back door man
sugar for your bowl
a hootchie coochie dream
call me sweet man in the night
call me freight train in the morning
call me harmonica weeping
call me St. Jamestown Infirmary
call me long gone and soon to come
the honky tonk river
a crossroads juke joint

I take pain and poison
 and turned them into art
I steal prayer and passion
 and hide them in my heart

Lawdy, Lawdy, Lawdy
blues been tattooed on my skin
sugar and sorrow sweeten my tears
Lead Belly was my doctor
Robert Johnson left me his mojo hand
I am yellow pin stripes
in a smokey room
hot sauce on pig ears
indigo flames licking
at the hunger in your hips
call me straight razor rage
call me cooling board regret
call me your heartbeat bass
call me the smell of chitterlings and sin
call me private lover and public pain
the first funkateer
the voice of aching midnight
our oldest self speaking
in quivering guitar squalls
call me honeysuckle ice cream
call me the chinky pin man
call me the first one
the one standing
knee deep in hell
shouting these low down
dirty
mean and evil blues

Elegy for the Crips
A Poem for the Street Gangs of L.A.

O city of crippled angels
city of electronic bantustans
O Watts O Compton O Inglewatts
Disney's version of Nazi camps
down in the city of angels
the golden orange festers
reeks over-ripeness
beneath the lordly hills
innocence is rotting
down there in the city of angels
deep down where colored angels
and crippled angels dance
where useless wings
lie gutter-spattered and stained
by endless red tape
and only the tears
of dark broken women
can cleanse the feathers
or starch the wings
of angels molting in the city

Fly away angels, flee
O dark eyed angels of Watts, flee
O brown toned angels of el barrio, flee
O deep hued angels of the street, flee
before the social workers
drink yr blood, flee
before the preachers
chew away yr left wing, flee
before the teacher
devours the right, flee

O flee this place
where sullen dusty angels
flay ashy manacled elbows
trying to escape the horror
of being dark and wingless
forever

O city of lost angels weep
for all the crippled angels
black dreaded angels
angels without agents
illiterate angels
angels without
a sky hook or a slam dunk
unwelcome angels
where their Uncle Tom denies them
a key to the city
he declares them chronically illegal
and definitely not CALIFORNIA ANGELS

O city of nubile cherubs
doe eyed madonnas
sloe eyed child/woman
only twelve
already a crippled angel
deforming in her womb
a crypt, a coffin
for angels yet to fall

O aimless anguished angels
dark men pray for you
dark women ache for you
as you limp leg
from projects to prison
your shoulders bloody
where wings were torn
O city of the crypts
blood soaked boxes
for pastel angels
swathed in coroner sheets
angels airmailed to Jesus
from the city of crystal angels

From this city of favored angels
this city of privileged angels
this city of holy angels
Gucci clad tourists
keep glancing nervously toward the east
where a million angelic ears
are tuned to the zillion watt
bass speaker of the universe
the tinsel stars start to fall
as golden spirits rise
rise up
up above the lordly hills
where a chorus is forming
a plan unfolding
as if by plan
though tomorrow is not promised
promise launches their dreams
sails in their eyes
path and plane point higher
pure blood poured out coldly
crippled children erecting an alter

Kneeling under a blue choke hold
entreating the angel of mercy
to teach them how to fly

Fathers' Turn

Since Moynihan and Moyers turned daddy
into a semen stain
Since Spielberg and Goldberg turned daddy
into a celluloid sissy
Since warfare and welfare turned daddy
into a food stamp
ain't no where to turn
but back
        toward each other

So turn yr field holler
and yr jawbone
back
        toward our own self

Turn yr Malcolm-tongued self
back
Turn yr Nkrumah-eyed self
back
Turn yr Bird-souled self
back
Back towards circles of fire
        unbroken vows
        and daddy
The way I see it
ain't no way to turn
but back
        toward each other

So turn jelly roll and belly rub
        into a family circle
Turn Mississippi misery
        into a Mandinka legend
Turn
Turn loops into spirals
Turn back
to where the women struggle
Turn back
        and when yr children call
turn their heads around
        spinning, spiraling
        ever upward
Cause ain't no where to turn
cept back
        towards each other
where families hold fast to fathers
and fathers hold families fast

A Mythic Blend of Red, Black & Green
(for Marcus Garvey)

I. The Red

We were groggy
Punch drunk giants
A beaten people
Both knees in the mud
Bowed heads awaiting the axe
When from over the horizon
A voice like a ship's bell rang
And our commodore commanded
"Rise up, rise up, ye mighty race"
The dark collective ear
Heard this clear-tongued peal
Aching knees heeded the command
Swollen eyes strained to glimpse
A jet black eagle
Flash across the bloody sun

Marcus, we were witness to your flight
We mold your mask from memory
Cling to the tender tendrils of your reason
We stand and face east
Where the sun is collecting
Our blood in pale pink clouds
For the gentle red rain
To bathe our sticky eyes
Marcus, heartbeat of our secret soul
Bleed us with your holy claws
Transfuse us with flame
Send firestorms rushing through our veins
Transform us into one drop demons
Garveyite soldiers
Bloodied vets of the vampire wars
We eat your heart Marcus
And swim in the deep red river of your genius

II. The Black

We were obsidian dreamers
Sleeping on an onyx mountain
Our wasted blood coagulated
Into a rock of flesh
As black as Cecil Rhodes' heart
When out of the bleak night of our misery
A voice like thunder echoing
Around Kilimanjaro
Warned us
"Be reasonable, be reliable, be resolute"
Words that cracked the walls

We heard you Marcus
Master mason
Chiseling our monuments
From destiny's rubble
Your fire set the molten magma
Flowing like sweat from Satchmo's brow
Your tongue charted our hip mystiques
On an unfurled scroll of skin
Skin so black it ate the sunlight
Painted our lips an electric blue

We remember and rejoice
Because you etched determination in our palms
Then folded our hands into fists
Fists to strike the drums
And summon us to the alter
Where the gemstone of resistance
Is blessed and set in the armour
Of those who fight the dragon of despair
Marcus, blessed ancestor
Grand marshal of our dreams
Make us mountain men
Turn us into stones
Stones that dance and demand
Hurl us at the wicked
Cement us into walls
Walls that will seal
The evil in their white houses
We embrace your granite stature
And find shelter in your shadow

III. The Green

We were soggy hulls
With barnacled, encrusted spirits
Pickled in the bitterest brine
Our diviners could find no
Sweet water in the wellspring of our stolen past
Until out of the Jamaican Sea
Came a mysterious mist
A mist to rinse deceit from our ears
So we could hear water sprites sing
Though black and bloody
You are heir to a history
You have a home
Across the water
On that green gold coast

We have come to testify
You unleashed the water
Shaped the common cup
Collected dew and rain
To quench our terrible thirst
An African Aquarian
Spilling knowledge on barren ground
Marcus you have shown us
The fruited path leading
To that crystal river
The river that runs
To the jade Atlantic
And the patinaed shores of home
Marcus, you are the pristine oasis
Amid the sandy dunes of fear
We gather around
Our sacred spout
With reverent lips
We sip the holy water
Of your relentless will

IV. The Blend

Rejoice we are blood
Rejoice we are stone
Rejoice we are water
We are red, black and green
The faithful colored race
Gathered on Babylon's shore
Certain that over the horizon
Out where stars stain the sea
There sails an African ark
A Black Star Liner
With Marcus at the helm
Soon he will ring
The star ship's bell
The moon will lower a stairway
We will march on board
Weigh anchor
And set sail for home

A Stool for Askia
(in honor of Askia M. Touré)

A stool for you, Askia
no watch, no plaque
no bogus proclamation
A stool, a tree rooted
in the salty soil of tradition
A stool, a seat that speaks
to our saner selves
and echoes like drums of old Memphis
A stool for Askia
our cultural comrade
soldier of struggle
His songs are swords of steel

A stool for you, Askia
for you have been our tongue
Without you we are mute
and mindless
You make Egypt young
You revive our old gods
and remind us of our
African home training
A stool for Askia
grizzled veteran of the freedom wars
Your deeds sear us
with their fierceness

A stool for you, Askia
We can feel fires
older than Kush
fueling your griotic memory
We all bear witness
to the flaming tears
in your Kemetic eyes
A stool for Askia
destiny's slowwalker
fluent in jackal and sphinx

A stool for you, Askia
We offer it and rejoice
because the wisdom seeker
has come to sit among us
His thoughts serpentine
and deep like the two Niles
He is the double faced gris-gris
His heart knows three worlds
His tongue mixes bebop with Bantu
His breath reeks of ritual
and revolt
A stool for Askia
'cause the truth teller
has come to treat our illness
and the faith keeper
has come to wake the dead

Yes! A stool for you, Askia
'cause you teach us songs
that take us back to Waset
You make us swim
in the waters of heritage
A stool for Askia
for he is testament
to our oldest, truest, wisest self

A stool to hail Askia
the namesake of old kings
for your treasured bone and breath
welds us to a hundred centuries
of unbroken blood
Your vision shields us from ignorance
You carry old world glory
on the spear of your tongue
You have tested the sacred science
of wood and word, worship and wisdom

A stool for you, Askia
freedom seeking
truth speaking
faith keeping soul singer
Come sit among us
Sing the songs that sanctify
Preach the poems that purify
Rap the rap of righteous reason
Raise us up
Re-civilize us
We have carved this stool
from awakened memories
Accept this stool
and we will emboss it
with hieroglyphics,
scarab and saxophone

About A Woman

Fire and lions
in the middle of my heart
a stammer on my lips
a smiling sphinx
in the middle of my war dance
You should know by now
that this is a poem about a woman

Go and stay
in the middle of my head
a flutter in my eye
a tear framed
in the middle of my lens
Now you know
this is a poem about a woman

Raisins and pineapples
in the center of my mouth
a feast in the circle of my arms
a marmalade butterfly
in the middle of my horror film
Yeah, you know
this is a poem about a woman

Clock and bomb
in the middle of my loins
a ticking in my head
a horn of plenty
in the middle of my bed
You know
this is a poem about a woman
a woman who will be there
at daybreak
holding her half of the sky

BeBop

BE BOP BE BOP BE BOP
BOP BOP BE BE BE BOP

begin with Bird
        blowing swing out of the box
Bird brain-storming
        with a chicken bone and a reed
Bird breathing blue badness
beating down beats chops
hipping the hipsters
to E flat pig latin
oob-blee splee bop

BE BOP BE BOP BE BOP
BOP BOP BE BE BE BOP

be bewitched by Miles
cause Miles be then
        Miles be now
        Miles be always
Miles be an Ogunian sky walker
a cool blue straight ahead hoodoo man
his axe be a sacred assan
listen and be possessed
by the Mississippi growling
thru St. Louis nights
Miles be Bantu prince
        be spitting raw rice
        be singing all blues
        be cool blues
be sketching Spain in dual hues
belongs to the brotherhood of blood
be straight ahead
for miles and miles and miles
over years and years and years
his raspy voice will be
and his muted horn will be
will be in our face
asking
so what?

BE BOP BE BOP BE BOP
BOP BOP BE BE BE BOP

be hip to the Max
cause Max has got elephant ears
and a Delta Blues heart
muddy water in his veins
he's got monkey feet
smoke stack lightning
in his hand
in his hand
Max Max Max
he strikes the drumhead
and demands
and demands
freedom freedom
sweet freedom now

BE BOP BE BOP BE BOP
BOP BOP BE BE BE BOP

be Thelonius bringing ivory
justice to bright Mississippi
smear ash and sweat
on the keyboards
straight no chaser
straight no chaser
and if the spirit moves you
get up and dance, dance
be a Thelonius Sphere
a sphere aspinning
a halo hovering
over sweaty piano dance
spin Sphere spin
spin rainbows for our ears
and when the spirit moves us
we will listen
and be Thelonious green
be Sphere red
be blue
be deep blue Monk!

BE BOP BE BOP BE BOP
BOP BOP BE BE BE BOP

be bopping like Dizzy
cause Diz hides Tunisian nights
in his beard
keeps salt peanuts
in his beret
bends his horn
toward heaven
so Joshua and Gabriel
can dig on bebop too

BE BOP BE POP BE BOP
BE BE BE BOP BOP BOP
BOP DE BE OPLEE SPLEEEEEEEE

Blood Bytes
(the path and tree commands)

they load us onto hard disk
crunch clipper ship cargo
into silicon giga bytes
cut and paste our spirituals
image write our welfare checks
laser print our food stamps
store our numbers on floppy disks
as supple as brain tissue

they commission fancy menus
encrypt the hidden files
and observe password security
while we must remember
the equality conditional test
requires two equal symbols
to represent equality
if equal equals word star
go to word star land
but if equal equals lotus
go to lotus land
confused? go to quit
word star land
word star
lotus land
lotus
quit
echo on the "not" option
go to worthless
then try batchprogramming
and utilize replaceable parameters
resort to conditional loops
distinguish between
random access memory
and last night's nightmare
echo worthless
pause

enter blood
okay echo
load blood
okay welcome aboard
mace utilities
strike any key
blood is loaded
every file glows red
and there is no limit
to the number of batch files
that can be chained together
subcommand go to lotus land
black foreground red background
red foreground black background
escape sequences strung together
byte by byte echo blood
echo blood batched
filed and chained
echo free echo invalid password
god in god out
strike any key
blood in god out
god in blood out
hi tech sacraments
okay holy communion
load bloody eucharist
echo hocus pocus
if equal equals mumbo jumbo
go to voodoo land
confused?
go to nonsense
go to worthless
go to quit!

Day Dreams

there are days
when it hurts to stay
and i'm afraid to go
so i crawl around
the closets of myself
trying to remember
where i stashed the dreams

there are days
when all my words
are dangerous
and all my actions offend
so i move about on tiptoe
and tremble when i speak
when best intentions
turn to ashes
and every thought
draws blood
my past mistakes
sit outside the door
and snicker
when i come
and go

there are days
when my friends
and my enemies
don the same uniforms
play the same games
trap me in the backcourt
with no one
to pass to

there are days when radio
and telephone
collaborate their lies
and i discover
that loneliness has keys
to all my doors

but there are moments
moments so pure
and promise filled
that on most days
i suffer sweet amnesia
and will dream
on a moment's notice

Deft Threat
(for our Colored Candidates)

Who speaks for the people?
Who will raise our spirit up?
Who will lay our enemy low?
You in the diamond limo
from your favored position
around the slop trough
can you see our eyes
full of questions?
Amid your squeals and grunts
can you hear our screams?
Can you forget our pain?

Reverend, Your Honor, Dr. Hamhock
what have you got to show
for all our daring deeds
and all our desperate deaths
Why are you denying your blood?
Brains of brie and beaujolais
no-singing, no-dancing robots
Souls fashioned from gold plastic
and microchips

You sit on the stool
carved from our bones
and glued with our knowledge
You have stolen our education
and squandered it on a German
car and Japanese contempt

We who are down pressed
We who are hungry, homeless, helpless
need to hear from you
need you to tell us
        Where is our voice?
        Where is our beauty?
        Where is our future?
What ever became of
        each one teach one?
Why are the teachers pushin' drugs?
Our scholars recommending ritalin
and writing inane dissertations
for the hyper-active and the brain-dead
full of bogus reasoning and lame excuses
PH.D.s in kissing the ass
of a dying cult
We who are illiterate
We who are denied, detained and demeaned
want to know
        Where is our learning?
        Where is our genius?
        Where is our Kuumba?

With Schwerner, Chaney and Goodman's
blood we mark our ballots
for the neo-segregationists
who pander for favor
like shine boys after tips
price tags stapled to their tongues
for rent posters plastered
to their backsides
Nervous sweaty people
with our silver in their pockets
and our future on their plates

We who have nothing
We who have been
signed, sealed and sold
need a clue
    Where are our jobs?
    Where are our homes?
    Where is our hope?

We did not ask these pretenders
    to speak for us
Grandslam, dunk, hit record freaks
Ebony/Jet centerfolds hyping
eleven billion dollars in hair grease
We who are faceless
    placeless and almost invisible
ask you, your celebrity superstarness
    Where are our heroes
        and sheroes?
    Where is our love
        and respect?
    Where is our revered reflection?

We who have we been 'buked
    and scorned
want to know
    Where is our ancestors' libation?
    Where is our drum/dance?
    Where is our spiritreach?

Your Honor, Reverend, Doctor Pork Chop
Greasy down presser pressing down
against the pressure
of our bloody uprising
Soon the betrayals
will fold in on each other
until once more revolt
proves real and rational
and in that sanctified season
we will stand and speaking
in one voice
we will say enough is enough
We will shape our questions
syllable by syllable

We will no longer teach you
        of our patience
        and our humility
We will not fatten you
        with our blood
We will not pray
        with or for you
And we will not
        let peace be still
until you who have grown
fat from our suffering
can answer
        Where is our kingdom?
        Where is our power?
        Where is our glory?

Elegy for the Seventh Son

I.
Even after he had fallen
he hung over the hall
like smoke hung over Watts
and his sacred blood stained
the fabric of our minds
For once again we mourned
became acolytes
in an American rite
agents in a morality play
We were adders and asps
frogs and snakes
all come to the ballroom
the icy Audubon ballroom
to witness him hang like
smoke over Capetown

And we are frozen in February
an eternal Audubon audience
repeated witness
as all shades of red are shattered
and scattered about the stage
like shards of scarlet glass
Where have we been
and what have we done
since our bright and flaming star
lay like liquid glass
red in all hues
scattered about the stage
St. Malcolm fallen and risen
and none of us with courage enough
to canonize the people's prophet

O the mourners wept like crocodiles
Neo Africans swore revenge
but no one claimed the shoes
of our martyred saint
No one wants the shoes
of a martyred man

II.

All hues of man missing
The loss crammed our ears
and clogged our minds
He took his last breath
and flecked the air with seeds
tiny red stars
sparks for the fire
and we are left to smolder
with no one to warn us
when the chickens come home to roost
O the sky was pallid
a planet with no sun
on that holy day when Malcolm fell
fell in all hues of red
was shattered and scattered
about the Audubon stage
like shards of scarlet glass
Pieces of Detroit Red, Dirty Red, Dago Red
each horrified by another Good Friday
An instant of agony from Angola Red
to Zulu Red
each cut by liquid glass
Shards from our bravest mirror
red in all hues
silent on the stage
electric in the air

O the mourners wept like crocodiles
the Mystics organized a cult
'cause its easy to worship a cold dead man
It's easy to worship a martyred man

III. FLASHBACK

Mrs. Little could see the future
and the future was red
First it was them night riders
tiny night riders
in the corner of her eye
gnats in the middle of her day
omens to bring her husband back
from across the bloody tracks
And little Malcolm Little
born fiery red

She slept among the harpies
night riders that buzzed like gnats
the bloody rails bearing a bleeding reverend
And little Malcolm Little fiery red
red jelly on his mouth
red sun in this eyes
His playground blood dripping
on white kitchen tile
The reds bothered her
until she made up her mind
to make her mind
a pane of coral tinted glass

She trapped all her demons
in the thin red mirror of her person
and then like a man swinging a hammer
she deliberately smashed the pane
and scattered her royal mind
like dust from an exploded ruby

O her neighbors wept like crocodiles
and sought an orphanage for her children
but we must not forget
that a crazy woman gave birth to a mighty man
A crazy woman gave birth to a martyred man

IV.

So mama went crazy and papa dead in hell
little wonder that little Malcolm grew
into a bright red devil
with a mind as caustic as conked hair
A plague from Detroit to Boston
Little red rider turned big red robber
A big fiery demon
a lava flow of rage
a molten wolfman
locked down in chain gang hell

He found a scarlet seed in a red bound book
He chewed every page like it was a bar on his cell
and then he sat waiting....
Waiting until little bitty Elijah Poole
part Garvey and part Daddy Grace
took red clay wisdom and remade himself
into the Honorable Elijah Mohammed
to whom all praise is due
all praise is due
because he reached down into hell
where a dangerous red devil was devouring
books
And using Georgia mother wit
Elijah delivered the people's flaming saint
Malcolm Little was a devil
Malcolm X was a phoenix aflame
He rose like a splinter
from flint and steel
and where Malcolm reasoned
we followed like sparks on a comet's tail

Minister Malcolm spoke and we heard
about devils and due
about cleaning up and rising up
Brother Malcolm began to raise the dead
and when he was his brightest
he was shattered and scattered about the
ballroom
like shards of glass
red in all hues

O the mourners wept like crocodiles
pretenders said that they knew him well
'cause it is easy to forget the truth about a
martyred man
It's easy to forget the truth about a martyred man

V.
The X could not contain the great fox
Separating eagles from chickens
Minister Malcolm gave devils names
He placed hell on the map
and taught us how spades were dealt
all in the name of Allah and Elijah
his prophet to whom all praise is due

The X could not name him
when he spoke
liars blushed
He delivered the messenger's message
Clean up, rise up, remember the past
so that we may act in the present
to shape the future
Clean up, rise up, remember the past
so that we may act in the present
to shape the future

His tongue was red pepper challenge
"If a man raises his hand to you
let him be prepared to lay down his life"
O he was ours in all his brightness
a red arrow tracking the racist heart
ballots for bullets
giving reason to rhyme
Malcolm, we didn't know your worth
until you were shattered and scattered
shards of deep red glass
splashing on the Audubon stage

O the mourners wept like crocodiles
claimed his courage for their own
remember it is easy to befriend a martyred man
It is so easy to befriend a martyred man

VI.
El Hadj Malik El Shabazz
a humble muslim
traveled from Mecca to Accra
tasting the coca and cola of Nkrumah's liberty
Over there in the once shameful jungle
he found genetic links with griots and gris-gris

He sat on a stool
as healers and sages
came and laid hands upon him
Each took a piece of him
until the chips of himself
were scattered about the room
like sunbeams along the veldt
When the sun had set
spirits came and gathered him up
and spoke to him in voices full of snakes
They asked, "Are you little red Malcolm Little,
Minister Malcolm X, El Hadj Malik El Shabazz?"
And our red self answered, "I am yours in all my
names."
Then beautiful and curious women
marveled at his color and asked,
"Were you born in hell?"
And our brave self answered,
"I am the color of flame
and yours in all my names
and yours in all my faces."

He rose like a rouge eagle
and all his fear and doubt was scattered
like shards of red stained glass
spangling a ballroom stage

O the mourners wept like crocodiles
glib men claim his as a son
'cause Malcolm was among us
Malcolm is with us
Malcolm will endure
for he is legend and longer
the wafer for our sins
Though he sits in the company
of Che, Geronimo and Lumumba
still he is here flecking the air
with dust from crushed jewels
He is the crimson in the baby's skin
the red eye of our sorrow
the glowing coal of our anger
We are a relentless river
he is the under tow
Our bond is seamless
He lives in our every righteous act
although he was shattered and scattered
slivers of red in all hues
he is ours and our bond is seamless
a song we have not sung
he is the color red
and ours
from first tint of daybreak
to the last flame of sunset
El Hadj Malik El Shabazz
your enemies were ours
El Hadj Malik El Shabazz
our enemies are yours
El Hadj Malik El Shabazz
our bond is seamless
for you are ours in all your names
and all your faces
'cause they will never destroy
the legacy of this martyred man
(Say it with me)
They will never destroy
the legacy of this martyred man....

For Howling Wolf

a feral wolf
fatigued by the forest rigors
sneaked into a farmhouse
lay down by the hearth
pretended to be a dog

he covered his fangs
softened his lupine smile
swapped the smell of fresh kill
for the stench of dead meat
traded freedom for comfort
throttled his growls
even fetched

he earned every ear scratch
every head pat
every table scrap
learned to wag his tail
and bark
started sleeping indoors
ignoring the calls of wild comrades
he wore a studded collar
grew partial to malamute bitches
and imported biscuits
'cause acting like a dog
seemed easier than living like a wolf

the wolf in dog's clothing
the dog in wolf's clothing
a divided soul
cursing the demanding moon

wolf-dog, dog-wolf
dog-dog, wolf-wolf
dog-wolf,
        HOWL

Georgia Peach Blues

I'm a Georgia Peach, come pick me
from the trees
I'm a Georgia Peach, you can pick me
from the tree
I'm ripe and ready to show
how sweet a Georgia Peach can be

I'm a Georgia Peach, I hang low down
on the vine
I'm a Georgia Peach, I hang low down
on the vine
And you ain't never tasted sweet peaches
until you've had the Georgia kind

I'm a Georgia Peach with a pit
as hard as stone
I'm a Georgia Peach with a pit
as hard as stone
But the flesh is sweet and tender
right down to the bone

I want you to squeeze me until the juice
runs down my leg
Squeeze me woman til the juice
runs down my leg
Come on and peel my peaches and
please don't make me beg

I'm a Georgia Peach and every night I dream
I'm a Georgia Peach and every night I dream
I dream that you'll come along
and dip me in your cream

I'm a sweet red peach, bake me in your pie
A red Georgia Peach, please use me in your pie
Put me in your oven and turn the heat up high
Cause you love peaches, I know you do
Cause you love peaches, I know you do
I've been saving this juicy fruit just
for you

Girl on a Crack

she looked like she was flying
sprawled in sand neath the swaying swing
she looked like an Ernie Barnes painting
cept she was dead neath the swaying swing

she would have been moved by the shimmering
of shadows across her sun-stained skirt
cause she always had an eye for balance
and tone and texture, that is until she cracked

until she was baptized in flame
a flashfire purging of Pollyanna's pipe dream
stoned on the rock that cracked her skull
and left her feeling sanctified and saved

until she was licked by tongues of fire
and made convert to the cloudy cult
of the scarred kneed, bleary eyed whores
who trade flesh for smoke

a charmed, star-crossed child woman
whose happiest hour
was one recess in 3rd grade
when she had ridden her creaking swing
out past the rim of the world
and peeped over the edge
at a woman sprawled cross a jagged crack

like some spawning creature
she returned at recess
smashed her blood stained pipe
rode her 3rd grade swing
up to the rim of the world
where
she would become the woman on the crack

Holiday

I.
Georgia January pale sunlight
streaking pink polished marble
demarking the designated demonstration stage
as deaf, dumb and docile media creations
and self-elected grand potentates
follow the perpetual widow around
and around the empty grave
pausing for photo opportunities
before their postcard crypt

While the guileless and guiltless
glean garbage for their feast
and celebrate in cardboard castles
certain that Martin is not on holiday
because they have seen him
huddled under a viaduct
sharing the warmth of a rusty barrel
listening to a drunken quartet sing

Coretta, Coretta
What has gone wrong
Coretta, Coretta
What has gone wrong
Ain't had no loving
since he been gone

II.
On bitter sweet Auburn Avenue
from inside Ebenezer Baptist
hollow bells herald
a poseurs' pilgrimage
to the theatre of greed and guilt
produced by Coors and Seagrams
written by Jesse Helms
and starring the US president
a morality play
to remind us
that the dead stay dead
but our fallen brother
our martyred Martin
shuns these heathen rites
where the ghoulish and the glib
bicker over recording rights
to *we shall overcome*
and turn this shared dream
into a fried chicken commercial

St Martin walks with paupers
along bloody boulevards
burdened with his name
where crack crazed women sing

Coretta, Coretta
Where you been so long
Coretta, Coretta
Where you been so long
We ain't had no loving
since he been gone

III.

Smiling and waving
pretend protesters parade
deceit on their lips
stumbling through vagrant-free zones
tone deaf amnesia victims
and corporate systemazoids
self-ordained spokepersons

Frolicking under cement peachtrees
the unwelcome and uninvited
recognize their scam
because we know the difference
between parading and marching

Our dreaming drum major
taught us the difference
between parody and protest
the difference between
nonviolence and nonsense
between compromise and capitulation
we search their powdered faces
for rhythm or blues
but they shuffle out of sight
in time for action news
so we can be eye witnesses
to pigs that don tail coats
top hats and walk upright

While on winter's
wind bayonetted streets
a red eyed ragman
rummages through the refuse
and sings his holiday song

Coretta, Coretta
What has gone wrong
Coretta, Coretta
What has gone wrong
We ain't had no justice
since he been gone
Ain't had no justice
since he been gone

In Her Honor
(for Gwendolyn Brooks)

This woman of work and wonder
is a righteous rain and a fierce fog
She toils and dreams in our midst
carries water from many rivers

This urn of sacred rainbows
a wellspring of voices
a fountainhead of songs
this bubble, this branch, this brook
this prayer, this passion, this poet
this leeward bayou
this liquid logic
pumping love and legend
thru the people's heart
With ink and insight
she seeds our souls
salts our tears
and speaks our mind

If we respect our elders
we must embrace her
If we embrace our past
we must value her
If we value courage
we must drink her up
like communion wine
This life, this love, this legacy
this bilet doux
this breathing book
this black sea
this brownstone oracle
this boiling brook

If we harbor hope
we must shelter her
If we shelter our prophets
we must pay homage
to this hallowed headwater
this blessed
this beloved
Gwendolyn Brooks

Invocation
Old spirit/New song

Papa Legba make us liquid
pour us like libations
pour us round the pole
that is our portal back
salute the sacred drummers
send their voices after us
down the harmonic river
to that delta
where done been
meets gonna be
summon the saints and the Loa
the snake and the bull
meet us at the turnstile crossroads
weave us into Shango's
red red lightening shirt
make us the tongue that lies
the eye that winks
a dancing shadow
the stars glint
make us tear drops
on the face of spring
make us remember that
we are the river
we are the rock

Linen Love

we smooth the sheets
sketch a smile
        on morning's mouth
name the day
        in each other's honor
eat tiny kisses
        for breakfast
compare the metro section
        with the want ads
smear cream cheese and jelly
        over the sports

we stage old stories
        act new dreams
pile plywood on the walls
        sprinkle pastels over the floors
        and spill crumbs in the bed
all before noon

we nap with siamese breath
dream of dolphins
and the answer to
27 across
we wake
        then make
        the earth shiver and quake

we wrap the afternoon
        in a calico blanket
and make the bed
        a second time

Red
A Performance Poem

Props required: one vial of red liquid

(Hold up vial and read)
This blood is ours
Blood this is ours
We are soaked
in the salt and sorrow
of this blood

(Shake the red vial and study its properties)
Red cells, genetic bars
bits of brains
Seweto and Selma
are sister cities
All our deaths are similar
wasted blood interchangeable

(Pour the red liquid on the ground)
We are bled everywhere
But Dracula has a face
and a known address
This blood is ours
Blood, ours to spill, spend or savor

(Drink some of the red liquid)
Slash a throat
slice a wrist
this sacred communion
this royal river

(Hold red liquid up to light)
There is an ark
floating in this blood

Never Can Say Good-by

(for Larry Neal and all them race men)

yeah unhuh unhuh yeah
holler y'all holler
for the race man
always giant steps ahead
of the aesthetic police
smearing pig grease
all over they classics
we listen with hoodoo hearts
we watch through bebop shades
and savor yr luminous ghostness
in the jellyfish sting
of our melodic rage
yeah unhuh unhuh yeah
yeah man
space man
race man
blowing bebop on a pencil
conjuring our fierceness
you all the time
making they words
suit our souls
holler for his hoodoo
bebop ghostifying feelings
never can say good-by
to those slick signifiers
and deep dozens players
unhuh yeah
unhuh in the window
unhuh in the water
unhuh in the mirror
the hoodoo lives
moist on the tip
of our tongues
holler y'all holler
yeah unhuh unhuh yeah

Spirit Catcher I

Sit me down
in a blue mauve place
stretch me across
yr ivory canvas lap
stroke my cheek
with a sable brush
smear oil and water
on my chest
hum prismic paeans
blow melody over my damp skin
cast a shadow spell
splash my soul
on the wall
and leave it there to dry

Umoja II

Umoja
from finger to fist
the scattered gathered up
together we are God's heartbeat
separated we are the devil's plaything
we begin with one
one person
one principle
one purpose
Umoja Umoja Umoja
the 1st sacred lesson
a whole self
a complete community
one race, one nation
one species
let the death dancers die
we will live in solidarity
with birth, breath and beauty
Umoja from finger to fist
from link to chain
from arc to circle
us one
one us
all we
Umoja is our purpose
one river, one road
one life, one family
all Umoja
Umoja
uni-voiced
uni-visioned
universal Umoja
the 1st step
and the last

Pretorian Elegy

Southern Africa: Great Cape Buffalo
with bloody flank and frothing breath
still your heart
an end is near

Pretoria, a lingering fester
polluting the life blood
of this tiny planet
but even now
dark anti-bodies
mass to defend the land
soon the fever will break
and South Africa will be free
or South Africa will be no more
Deep in the mines
we feel the shudders
of African earth grunting in pain
for the fruit of her womb

Yet in Pretoria
pale impotent Pretoria
high seat of the south
pinup for apartheid
Pretoria, the final stronghold
for parchment cannibals
who pollute the earth with their undigested diets
of African minerals and African blood
nature and wise men are conspiring
and all the children know
that Biko is not dead
They have seen him
swap places with shadows
Some say he is
the people's red-eye panther

He is here and gone
a shaka ray and a star
Biko and all his unnamed brothers and sisters
are a song of victory
on the lips of a righteous force

The Pretorian sky darkens
as the people's tears
flow 'cross molten rage
creating electric clouds
Restlessness is about
Dark eyes frisk the sky
Thunder in the distance
speaks like a bass tambourine
The drum that used to talk
he say: Angola free
bosses in Pretoria say: never
Again the heavens' drummer speaks
say: Mozambique free now
White ladies tell their maids
it is a lie
but now the night
displays a blood red star
The elders welcome it
and claim it as a sign
Zimbabwe free
Pretoria newspapers deny it
and continue dealing in exotic imported Blacks
Sun City traitors raised in America
shameless men, honorary white men
who carry their work permits
tucked between the sheet music
and the closed deal

And always the persistent thunder
it say: Angola free
Black soul singer from New York City
are you for a free Pretoria?
The thundering skies
will not be silent

They say Mozambique is free
Dark ambassador from Georgia
what would you give for a free Pretoria?
Corporate lackey from the Ivy League
have you a deal
that will free Pretoria?
If not, take your comrades,
singers, athletes
deceivers and diplomats
Take them, leave quickly
and do not return
until your eyes are open
and you wear the freedom fighters' green

O brothers of the blood
O sister to the soul
our great black panther is aroused
The children need the land
Pretoria must be free
Brother man in London
knows it to be true
Pretoria must be free
The children need the land
The elders want their stools
Sister woman in Cuba
knows and she remembers the urge
Pretoria must be free

The children need the space
The elders want their place
The panther, lean and justice starved
stalks freedom in Pretoria
and nothing can deter
nine-hundred million panther cells
united, demanding an answer
For Pretoria must answer
for its abominations
for its arrogance
and for its evil alliances
with torture, death and Nestle's chocolate

The babies know the way
Our pulses know the truth
a dark diaspora spinning
like melanic hemoglobin
coagulating into the iron will
that screams for freedom, freedom now

For once I longed to touch
a blade of grass
in spring
in a park
in Pretoria
in peace
"UH....YES SIR BOSS
I GOT ME PASS, RIGHT HERE!"

Sunday Morning Southern Church

The words
liquid feathers of owls
whipped and churned
by satin tongues
in skulls of mother wit

The sermon
summons fried chicken dreams
and peach flavored hopes
for grandma's spirit
She waits
til she gets to heaven

The hymns
fragile glassine magic
all the meaning crushed
leaving goober dust cures
for next week's pain

The chant
a dance of dry bones
through checkered space
to where Martin wept
in Memphis, in Mecca
O Lord didn't it rain

The clap
coconut hands cupped
forming sanctified wombs
for a virgin rebirth
I've been born again

The choir
mountain top songs
from wingless birds
some glad morning
I shall fly away

The spirit
leaps from preacher eyes to
too tight Sunday shoes
Sister Sarah's got the spirit
O Lord she can't sit down

The ritual
rewards six day labor
with a someday dream
I do believe
we shall overcome one day

The faith
a fiery spring
bubbling under the bridge
over troubled water
where amazing grace
will ease a worried mind

Sunday morning
southern church
myth becomes the dragon
that swallows pain
and paradise is not lost...
let the church say Amen.

A Blues Poem
(for Langston Hughes)

First Beat

Say blues ain't nothing but a feeling
Say blues ain't nothing but a song
Say blues ain't nothing but a feeling
Say blues ain't nothing but a song
But I've had this mean old feeling
four hundred years too long

Blues crawled out of the sea
at Jamestown, playing castanets
carved from the ivory jaw bones
of those resting under an indigo blanket
in the deep slumber of the middle passage

The tempo quickened and merged
into chain jangling coffle rhythms
into bent back sweat sounds
into barefoot drums on big house floors
became a servant to survival

It turned to wind and whistles
through the green lips of dixie
wept tears yellow with age
for babies buried under rivers
yet kept the salty taste of blue

Second Beat

Say blues reached out and touched me
Reached out and touched my hand
Say blues reached out and touched me
Reached out and touched my hand
Say blues done come to save me
from this mean and evil land

The blues rode night trains north
smelling of yams and collard greens
carrying box lunch hopes
wearing Sunday go to meetin' dreams
trying to shed down home skin

It found a guitar pick in the snow
harmonica chords in slaughter houses
and a scream for lost fingers
chopped like cotton
by the wheels of industry

Stood shivering and cold
in icy unwanted lines
pleading for a handout
watching calloused fingertips
frozen a deeper blue

Third Beat

Say big old filthy city
Lawd I'm sick of you
Say big old filthy city
Lawd I'm sick of you
If it wasn't for the blues
don't know what I'd do

Blues hidden among suburban ham hocks
in greasy subway shopping bags
watching Aunt Jemima and Beulah
steal life for their children
on two dollars a week and bus fare

Saw zootsuit warriors, jilted
by hip shaking mamas
wept razor blade tears
at Saturday night rent parties
and Sunday morning jails

Ma Rainey and Bessie Smith
took a pig foot and a bottle of gin
gave tonic to a weary race
and a race music fortune
to Columbia Records

Fourth Beat

Say evil's 'bout to catch me
Even though I paid my dues
Say evil's 'bout to catch me
Even though I paid my dues
Luck ran off and left me
here to sing these blues

The blues put hope in mama's smile
and magic in her children's eyes
it blocked the bill collector's path
and hid an extra onion
in an empty cupboard

The blues is an eddy that swirls two ways
a tart crystal powder of past anguish
mixed into a creamy balm for future pain
blood shed and unshed, congealed
into four bar harmony

Blues comes at twilight
a wind that ruffles the feathers
of throatless ravens
perched on tenement window sills
listening for the hyena's laugh

Say blues ain't nothing but a feeling
Say blues ain't nothing but a song

Say blues ain't nothing but a feeling
Say blues ain't nothing but a song
But I've had this mean old feeling
four hundred years too long

Blackmusicman
(to Pharoah Saunders)

They call him Pharoah
but he ain't no ancient
Egyptian ruler, although
his essence is older than
the sphinx

He is tomorrow garbed
in the trappings of now
using fragments of sound
and space
like a precision laser
he blows holes in our here
giving glimpses of there
of everywhere

He is a mind surgeon
transplanting the seeds
of Turner, Vesey & Malcolm
behind black brows

Pharoah! Pha-ra-oh! Pharoah
squealing, screeching, screee-ming
Pharoah causing the spirits
of our ancestors and of our unborn
futures to marry in the air

Pharoah
time is his fingers
the past is his eyes
Ra the sun calls him son
and casts his shadow
across eons

Pharoah
a gris-gris man
sprinkling cosmic goober dust
in black ears
he is black sorcerer
mixing a magical music
that shows us the path to forever

Listen...
to the wind
it's Pharoah moaning
listen to the rain
the rhythm is him
feel the universe
crackle, reminding
us that Pharoah is
really is
is the smoke God
is black lighting
is Back unity
is!
    listen...
    to the wind
    it's Pharoah moaning...

On This Street

I have spent half my years
on this street where
daylight is an unwelcome intruder
lending an unhealthy brightness
to nights of dismal thoughts
and dawn interrupts a night song sang
by madmen who wrap themselves
in velvet and chant
lunatic lyrics to the closed
ears of radios

On this street where Jesus was evicted
because his mother's social worker
cut her check, she was living with a man
and red flashing light
administers extreme unction
for slain fortune hunters

On this street where children know
that life goes better with Coke
and that Eldorados are powered by
pedaled ass and steered by
turned tricks

On this street where blind mailmen
deliver dead letters to illiterates
who can only read the stars and
poppies grow from the forehead of
junked men who dream of finding
a baggie with a horse inside

I have spent half my years on
this street, I've smelled
the stench, tasted the wine,
heard the pain and seen the
blood. Yet I cannot leave
there are poems here

Ghetto

I.
Coal lump in the melting pot
that cannot dissolve
and will not sink
Looking glass reminder
of a would be diamond
Blues tinted wasteland
encased in a siren dome

Where night trains pass
on cocaine tracks
as shivering men
under midnight quilts
lean in doorways
waiting
to snuff tomorrow
up their nose

Where someone's baby sister's
hip sways thru a timeless alley
gliding over the last lyric
of grandma's death song
selling plots of fertile space
to pawn brokers of satin thighs

Where store front temples
recruit Christian soldiers
to stamp out creativity
and castrated athletes
dribble celluloid basketballs
thru piss-stained movie houses
trying to fake reality
and score

Where fratricide, suicide and genocide
practice medicine in free clinics
and winos become blood bankers
pumping red life and legend
into plastic tubes
to feed crazed vampires

Where school wardens steal
six year old genius
and starving children are molested
by food commercials
Where the knees of dreamers
grow calloused from begging
for ballot boxes
to ring up three lemons
begging for relief lines
to issue land and mules
begging for a job
for justice
and for Jesus to come back
and take his medicine
like a man

II.
Despite wailing and despair
jade tears mark our graves
time and pressure
will turn coal into diamonds
for we carry snow, rain
and sea shells
in our pockets

We carry Sunday in our hearts
and music in our blood
We are an echo of tomorrow
the shadow of forty centuries gone
We are the magic
that leaped thru the eyes of Antar
and taught him the dance of war
We brought fire to Europe
and rain to the Sahara
We ruled Atlantis
gave mathematics to Mu
and medicine to Imanhoteph
We have conversed with Ra
counseled pharaohs
created undiscovered dreams
hung Vega around our neck
We built the zodiac
then rested for a great year
quick silver blood
teardrop and rainbow
pulsating thru polished mahogany
lion jaws on gazelle paws
eagles screaming thru shark teeth
music seen in dew drops
the south wind calling
to a volcanic lover
We are giants trapped in space
We are Africa with amnesia
forever without a clock.....

Don't Ask

how about them democrats
how about them republicans
how about them terrorists
and how about that desert storm
and how about them homeless
them hungry
them hopeless
singing the same old song
ever since slavery time
they gets the meat
and we gets the rind
they gets the meat
and we gets the rind
how about that election
huh?...huh?...huh?

what about your word
and what about your honor
and what about in god we trust
and what about the rest of us
what about them inside buys
them treaties
them spies
seems this is the way its gotta be
i lie to you
cause you lied to me
i lie to you
cause you lied to me
what about all them red lines
huh?...huh?... huh?

and how come no one can say gerrymandering
with a straight face
how come the haves have
and how come the nots don't dig it
who decided all these decisions
and who said they could
who asked us to be citizens
and who said we would
who are these dreamers
who keep waking us up
who is gonna play Malcolm this time
seems the way it's always been
if we don't stand together
we don't stand to win
if we don't stand together
we don't plan to win
who is this apathy anyway
huh?...huh?...huh?

although it's not my task
old spirits make me ask
how about this planet
how about these people
how about this poem?

the author:

Robert Earl Price is Playwright-in-Residence at 7Stages Theater, Atlanta, GA. His passionate lyrical style has garnered the praise of authors Toni Morrison and Gwendolyn Brooks and earned writing credits in almost every literary genre. Robert Earl has been a National Endowment for the Arts Literary Fellow chosen for poetry which has appeared in scores of magazines, journals and anthologies as well as two books: **Blood Lines** and **Blood Elegy**.